DC COMICS™

SUPERMAN™
SCIENCE

SOARING THE SKIES

SUPERMAN™ AND THE SCIENCE OF FLIGHT

BY *TAMMY ENZ*

SUPERMAN CREATED BY
JERRY SIEGEL
AND **JOE SHUSTER**
BY SPECIAL ARRANGEMENT
WITH THE JERRY SIEGEL FAMILY

Published by Curious Fox, an imprint of Capstone Global Library Limited, 7 Pilgrim Street, London, EC4V 6LB – Registered company number: 6695582

www.curious-fox.com

STAR37775

Edited by Christopher Harbo
Designed by Bob Lentz
Production by Tori Abraham
Picture research by Eric Gohl
Originated by Capstone Global Librar
Printed and bound in China

ISBN 978 1 78202 496 5
20 19 18 17 16
10 9 8 7 6 5 4 3 2 1

British Library Cataloguing in Publication Data
A full catalogue record for this book is available from the British Library

Awknowledgements
DVIDS: Staff Sgt. Jonathan Snyder, 26 (bottom); iStockphoto: Joe_Potato, 9 (top), Vasily Smirnov, 28; Library of Congress: 8, 10 (all); NASA: 29, Tony Landis, 25 (top); National Archives and Records Administration: 11; Shutterstock: Al Mueller, 19 (bottom), Aleksei Lazukov, 13 (top), Alexandra Lande, 12, Andrey Khachatryan, 25 (bottom), Attila Jandi, 18, Betto Rodrigues, 15, Boykov, 23 (bottom), Christian Mueller, 9 (bottom), Daniel Huebner, 16, eddtoro, 14, Ensuper, cover, FloridaStock, 7 (bottom), Jari Sokka, 20 (top), Lee Yiu Tung, 17 (right), Lu Yao, 27, Mariia Tagirova, 21, muratart, 7 (top), OPIS Zagreb, 24, Peter Vrabel, 20 (bottom), Ryan M. Bolton, 17 (bottom left), Sindre T, 13 (bottom), Tony Campbell, 17 (top left), Werner Lehmann, 19 (top); USAF: 23 (top), TSgt. Effrain Lopez, 26 (top), TSgt. Michael Haggerty, 22

INTRODUCTION
UP, UP AND AWAY! 4

SECTION 1
FLIGHT LESSONS 6

SECTION 2
HUMAN HIGH-FLIERS 10

SECTION 3
ALIENS AMONG US 16

SECTION 4
WONDERS IN
MODERN FLIGHT 22

GLOSSARY 30

READ MORE 31

WEBSITES 31

INDEX 32

UP, UP AND AWAY!

     With an effortless leap, Superman bounds into the air. No wings. No engines. No special gear or gadgets. Just a cape and his unique ability to defy the scientific laws that keep us grounded. Imagine what it would be like to have his power of flight. Where would you go? What would you see?

     For thousands of years, flight really was something people could only dream about. But these days, soaring the skies is not limited to superheroes. While we lack the Man of Steel's superpowers, the ability to fly is well within our grasp. In fact, we often take it for granted. Almost anywhere on this planet is just a plane ride away.

     But have you ever stopped to think about what makes flight possible? For instance, how does a hang-glider stay aloft with no engine to power it? Or what helps a massive jumbo jet get off the ground? The answers are simple: science, engineering and a little inspiration from nature. From wingsuits and fighter jets to flying fish and stealth aircraft, get ready to explore the incredible world of flight.

FACT:

When Superman first appeared in comics in 1938, he could leap great distances and over tall buildings. It wasn't until the early 1940s that he was shown to actually fly.

FLIGHT LESSONS

One second Clark Kent peels off his shirt and tie. The next, Superman soars over Metropolis. Flight is child's play for Superman, but it challenged scientists and engineers for centuries. Now their discoveries in flight science allow us to touch the clouds.

THE PHYSICS OF FLIGHT

Flight takes many forms. Birds flap their wings and aeroplanes use jet engines. But both must deal with gravity. Gravity is the force that pulls all objects towards Earth. Everything dropped, launched or flown falls to Earth unless it overcomes gravity. To do that, fliers must employ **thrust** to move them forward through the air. Aircraft get thrust from their powerful engines. Birds experience thrust when they flap their wings.

But forward thrust alone won't keep fliers airborne. They must also create **lift**, or an upward force, to overcome gravity. Birds and planes have shaped wings to help create lift, but they only work when moving. An aeroplane doesn't create lift if its engines fail to push it forwards. And while birds can glide without flapping, gravity pulls them down as their thrust decreases.

Commercial jets use powerful engines and shaped wings to achieve the thrust and lift necessary for lift-off.

LOW ENERGY LIFT

Eagles and other birds of prey are experts at creating lift with little effort. Their heavy bodies make flapping tiring. Instead, these birds seek out **thermal** currents. Without flapping, they ride rising pockets of warm air upwards for hundreds of metres.

AERODYNAMIC AIRFOIL

Does Superman's cape hold the secret to his flight powers? No. But the way it cuts through the air might just give the Man of Steel a little extra lift. In the real world, the shape of an aeroplane's wings is the key to staying airborne.

Otto Lilienthal with one of his gliders in 1895

The design of the modern aeroplane wing dates back more than 120 years. In the 1890s, bird wings inspired German engineer Otto Lilienthal to experiment with **airfoils**. An airfoil is a gently curved blade shape that causes air to move quicker over its top than its bottom. This movement creates lower air pressure above the wing to suck it upwards. Meanwhile, the angle of the wing redirects air downwards. As air is pushed down, the wing experiences lift as it is pushed up.

FLAP

Flaps increase an airfoil's curve to improve lift during take-offs.

Staying aloft is one thing, but how does an airfoil help a heavy passenger jet take off? At take-off, pilots lower flaps on the back of a jet's wings. These flaps make the airfoil's curve larger to increase lift. At 258 to 290 kilometres (160 to 180 miles) per hour, enough lift is created to raise the jet. While flying, the flaps are retracted to reduce **air resistance**, or drag. This helps the plane to cruise at 885 to 933 kilometres (550 to 580 miles) per hour.

STOPPING POWER

Aircraft wings are shaped to reduce drag, but they also have features to increase it. Why? Because stopping a loaded plane landing at 240 kilometres (150 miles) per hour is no small feat. Jets need more than their brakes to stop. They also use spoilers. These wing flaps flip up to create more drag to help stop the plane.

SPOILER

airfoil   curved surface causing lift in flight

air resistance   force of air rubbing against things

HUMAN HIGH-FLIERS

Superman is a symbol of our desire to be better, stronger and faster. Likewise, his ability to soar the skies is a reminder of our long-held fascination with flight. And that fascination has led to some pretty amazing contraptions.

FOUNDERS OF FLIGHT

Dreams of human flight date back hundreds of years. In the 1400s, Leonardo da Vinci created more than 100 drawings that showed his ideas for flying machines. But it wasn't until the 1890s that human flight really took off. Otto Lilienthal's attempts to fly the first gliders inspired the scientists and engineers who eventually shaped the future of flight.

Two of those people were Orville and Wilbur Wright. Building on Lilienthal's ideas, the Wright brothers ushered in the era of powered flight. On 17 December 1903, their plane lifted off in Kitty Hawk, North Carolina, USA. It stayed aloft for just 12 seconds and only covered about 37 metres (120 feet). But that short hop changed flight forever.

Orville Wright

Wilbur Wright

Orville Wright flies one of his early planes at
Fort Myer, Virginia, USA, in September 1908.

In a few years, flight innovation skyrocketed. In 1914, planes
were used in World War I (1914–1918) spy missions. By the end of the
war they were being used for bombing runs and air combat. Not long
afterwards, overseas flight became a reality. On 14 June 1919, John
Alcock and Arthur Brown made the first non-stop flight across the
Atlantic. It took them 16 hours in a modified British Vimy bomber.

THE FIRST HELICOPTER

Igor Sikorsky developed the rotor designs for the first successful
mass-produced helicopter. His skeletal VS-300 took flight
on 14 September 1939. It made helicopter history by staying
airborne for a few seconds. But modern helicopters still use
Sikorsky's main rotor and tail rotor design today.

UNPOWERED FLIGHT

The Man of Steel flies completely unassisted. He punches through the clouds without jet engines or rocket boosters. Can humans do anything similar?

Human-powered flight has fascinated inventors for decades. And some have even achieved it. In 1979 Bryan Allen piloted the Gossamer Albatross across the English Channel. This 32-kilogram (70-pound) pedal-powered plane made the 36-kilogram (22.5-mile) flight in 2 hours and 49 minutes. To stay up, Allen pedalled non-stop.

Hang-gliders rely on rising pockets of air to stay airborne.

More commonly, people achieve unpowered flight with hang-gliders. These triangular airfoils produce lift with a running take-off from a hill or mountain. The glider then catches ridge and thermal lifts to gain **altitude**. Ridge lifts occur when air pushes upwards as wind hits a cliff. Thermal lifts are rising hot air pockets. Hang-gliders can stay aloft for hours at a time, soaring for hundreds of kilometres.

Wingsuiters may come the closest to feeling like Superman in flight. These daredevils jump from planes wearing suits with arm and leg flaps. The flaps catch air to allow wingsuiters to slow down and glide. While a skydiver reaches 193 kilometres (120 miles) per hour in free fall, wingsuiters fall at only 80 to 97 kilometres (50 to 60 miles) per hour. Slight body movements help wingsuiters steer and change direction in mid-flight. They release parachutes for safe landings.

wingsuit

A wingsuiter glides like a superhero high above the ground.

altitude   height of something above sea level or Earth's surface

Unpowered flight can only take humans so far. To really fly like Superman, scientists and engineers have stepped up the game with jet packs.

Military engineers began developing jet packs as early as the 1940s. By 1960, Bell Aerosystems produced the Bell Rocket Belt for the US Army. Fuelled by hydrogen peroxide, it was able to stay aloft for only 21 seconds. Although engineers tried changing it to jet power, the military eventually shelved their jet pack plans.

A Bell Rocket Belt 2 is on display at the National Air and Space Museum's Steven F. Udvar-Hazy Center in Virginia, USA.

Riders race above the waves with water-propelled jet packs.

More recently private tinkerers have taken up the quest for functional jet packs. In the early 2000s, Canadian Raymond Li developed a jet pack propelled by water. His Jetlev-Flyer produces up to 227 kilograms (500 pounds) of thrust to send riders soaring above the water.

Even more amazing are the flying feats of Swiss pilot Yves "Jetman" Rossy. He is famous for flying like an eagle by strapping on a rigid wing with four tiny jet engines. His 15-minute trips reach speeds of up to 306 kilometres (190 miles) per hour. His wings have taken him over the Alps and across the English Channel.

SPRINGTAIL EFV

Jetman Rossy may soon have to share his jet pack fame. The Springtail Exoskeleton Flying Vehicle (EFV) uses a single engine to power fan blades. This futuristic-looking craft can fly for two hours and reach a top speed of 182 kilometres (113 miles) per hour. It can also hover in place.

ALIENS AMONG US

Thrusting his arm skywards, Superman glides between skyscrapers, zooms across the globe and hovers at will. Obviously, he's not bound by our planet's laws of physics. But some Earth dwellers among us also appear to defy natural laws. Some animals perform unbelievable feats of flight.

ECCENTRIC ANIMALS

You'll find birds, insects and Superman in the sky. But do fish, squirrels and snakes stick to only water and land? Not all of them. Some amazing creatures break beyond their natural habitats.

Imagine seeing a flying fish soar past your boat at 60 kilometres (37 miles) per hour. Forty species of flying fish live in Earth's oceans. Their rapidly beating tails launch them from the sea to avoid predators. Using wing-like fins, they glide 1.2 metres (4 feet) above the water for up to 200 metres (655 feet) at a time. That's more than the length of two football pitches!

flying fish

Not to be outdone by ocean dwellers, a few unlikely land animals also take to the air. Flying squirrels use flaps between their front and back legs to soar up to 46 metres (150 feet) from tree to tree. Paradise tree snakes glide for up to 100 metres (330 feet) by flexing their bodies to sail through treetops. And Wallace's flying frogs glide through the jungles of Malaysia and Borneo using **membranes** between their toes and skin flaps on their sides.

flying squirrel

paradise tree snake

Wallace's flying frog

UNBELIEVABLE BIRDS

Flying to the other side of the world is a snap for Superman. In the real world, several bird species make comparable **migrations**. The Arctic tern travels from Greenland to Antarctica each year. This 71,000-kilometre (44,000-mile) trip zigzags across the Atlantic following favourable wind currents. Over its 30-year life span, the tern flies about 2.4 million kilometres (1.5 million miles). That's like flying to the Moon and back three times.

Arctic tern

sooty terns

The Arctic tern flies far, but the tropical sooty tern flies long. It stays airborne from the time it leaves the nest until it returns to lay eggs. Just how long is that? Up to five years! In flight, the sooty tern swoops down to pluck fish from water or to grab flying fish. And its shrill call sounds like "wide-a-wake". That's an apt call, as they sleep only a couple of seconds at a time in flight.

HUMMINGBIRD ACROBATICS

The ruby-throated hummingbird can't walk and can barely hop with its tiny legs. But it beats its wings 53 times each second to hover and fly upside down and backwards. It also eats twice its weight in food each day to have enough energy to accomplish these feats.

migration regular movement of animals as they search different places for food

AMAZING ARTHROPODS

Superman's flight powers are unexplainable. How does he take off unassisted? What keeps him in the air? But sometimes insect flight is equally mystifying.

Insect flight doesn't always follow the same rules as bird and plane flight. Tiny bumblebee wings don't look like airfoils. And they hardly look large enough to keep the bees aloft. But by fluttering incredibly fast, bumblebee wings create tiny vortexes. These low-pressure areas above the wings generate lift to keep the bee flying.

bumblebee

FACT:

The painted lady butterfly makes a 6,437-kilometre (4,000-mile) migration from North Africa to Iceland.

blowfly

The blowfly's flight is only understandable with the aid of high-powered X-ray technology. With this technology, scientists discovered that the fly uses muscles smaller than the width of human hair to beat its wings 150 times per second. These muscles are not attached directly to its wings. Instead they are inside the fly's **thorax**. As the fly changes the shape of its thorax, the movements are transferred to the wings.

ROBOBEE

Scientists from Harvard University in the United States have applied their knowledge of a fly's biology to create RoboBee. This tiny robot flaps its paper-thin wings 120 times per second. Future jobs for RoboBee could include crop pollination and search and rescue missions.

thorax middle section of an insect's body; wings and legs are attached to the thorax

WONDERS IN MODERN FLIGHT

Seeing the Man of Steel in flight naturally inspires us to want to fly higher and faster. But flight inventions have already achieved some amazing feats – and they're poised to go even higher.

INNOVATION IN FLIGHT

One secret to Superman's success is his ability to outsmart super-villains. Likewise, some of our greatest innovations in flight come from our need to out-think our enemies. It's no wonder the military is such a hotbed for flight innovation.

Spy and stealth planes are military specialities. The SR-71 Blackbird spy plane was one of the fastest planes ever built. It could fly more than 3,219 kilometres (2,000 miles) per hour. That's three times faster than the speed of sound. The aircraft was so fast, it was never hit by a missile in its 25 years of service.

SR-71 Blackbird

Speed is good for making fast getaways. But for sneaking up on an enemy you'll need the B-2 Spirit bomber. This 52-metre (172-foot) wide boomerang-shaped bomber is virtually undetectable. Its flat black shape and muffled engines keep it hidden in plain sight. More importantly, its composite skin and **radar**-absorbing paint make it look like an insect on radar scanners.

B-2 Spirit

JUMP JETS

Normal fighter jets need long runways for take-offs and landings. But the Harrier Jump Jet can take off like a helicopter and fly like a jet. Its revolving jet nozzles give it thrust to lift off short runways and small aircraft carriers. Harriers reach speeds of up to 1,175 kilometres (730 miles) per hour in flight.

CARGO CARRYING

Between his strength and his ability to fly, Superman makes his job look easy. After all, he can guide crashing passenger jets to the ground without breaking much of a sweat. In the real world, however, lifting cargo takes a huge effort – and a huge plane.

The largest cargo carrier in the world is the Russian Antonov An-225. From front to back and wing tip to wing tip, this beast is nearly the size of a football pitch. It can carry more than 226,800 kilograms (500,000 pounds), or the weight of about 50 elephants. It hauls anything up to 10 metres (33 feet) in diameter and 70 metres (230 feet) long. Loads that can't fit inside it can be carried on the An-225's back. All loaded up, it can still fly 800 kilometres (500 miles) per hour.

The nose of the An-225 flips up so that large cargo can be easily loaded.

Super Guppy

NASA's Super Guppy is another huge cargo carrier. The Guppy looks more like a fish than a plane. Its hinged nose opens to reveal a huge cargo bay. It can carry more than 23,680 kilograms (50,000 pounds) of cargo. Since 1962, this monster has played a vital role in the transportation of spacecraft parts.

TRANSPORT HELICOPTERS

Planes aren't the only heavy lifters. The Mi26 transport helicopter can easily hoist and carry a 737 jetliner. This massive chopper uses an eight-blade propeller. It can carry 18-tonne loads at 295 kilometres (183 miles) per hour.

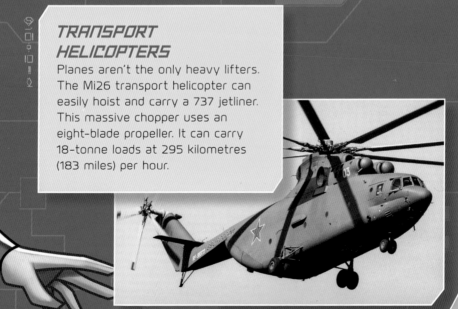

DRONES

When super-villains strike, the citizens of Metropolis can count on Superman to swoop in and save the day. In our world, we've discovered ways to sit back and let high fliers handle our toughest jobs. More unmanned aerial vehicles (UAVs) fly our skies today than at any other time in history.

Military UAVs are invaluable in sticky situations. Piloted by a crew many kilometres away, Reaper and Predator drones scout sites ahead of troops or manned vehicles. Pilots use onboard cameras to guide their flights. In the dark, infrared cameras give them night vision. Reapers and Predators help troops in battle by locating and destroying specific targets.

A Predator drone is controlled remotely by a pilot on the ground.

Recreational drones have built-in digital cameras to provide an eye in the sky.

Although military drones have been at work for years, drone use by ordinary people is rising quickly. Some experts think more than 30,000 drones will be flying overhead in the United States alone by 2020. Many owners use their personal drones for making films and taking photos. And companies are gearing up for drone use too. Agricultural companies have developed drones to help farmers check crop conditions on large farms. Estate agents use drones to film virtual tours of houses for sale. One company in the UK has even tested out drones for pizza delivery.

THE FIRST UAV

UAVs have been around since the 1860s. Charles Perley's aerial bomber was used in the American Civil War (1861–1865). This UAV was a hot air balloon loaded with explosives and a timing mechanism.

Superman can fly well beyond the upper reaches of the clouds. Whether guiding a nuclear warhead into space or flying to an alien planet, nothing holds him back. For humans, space flight was only a long-held dream for thousands of years. But now science and engineering give us the power to achieve those dreams.

For more than 50 years, rockets have been our ticket off Earth. They have delivered people to the Moon, robots to Mars and probes to the very edges of our solar system. While they come in many shapes and sizes, they all work in similar ways. Rockets burn fuel to produce hot gases. These gases expand and blast downwards to generate incredible thrust. To escape Earth's gravity, a rocket must reach a speed of 40,230 kilometres (25,000 miles) per hour.

Hot gases burst from the bottom of a rocket to thrust it skywards.

interstellar between stars; most often used to describe travel from one star to another

Travelling beyond our solar system is the next space hurdle. But that quest has already begun. In 1977, NASA launched the *Voyager 1* space probe. In 2012, it achieved **interstellar** flight when it reached the edge of our solar system. At its current speed, it would reach our nearest neighbouring star in 40,000 years. Unfortunately, *Voyager 1* is expected to run out of fuel around 2025, long before it ever gets there.

An artist's impression of *Voyager 1* flying through space.

CONCLUSION

No human invention can compete with Superman's command of the skies. He can fly nearly anywhere in the blink of an eye and land with hardly a hair out of place. While we are awed by his grace, science and engineering can still give us a taste of his abilities. From robot bees and massive cargo jets to wingsuits and hang-gliders, the science of flight helps us soar.

GLOSSARY

airfoil curved surface causing lift in flight

air resistance force of air rubbing against things

altitude height of something above sea level or Earth's surface

interstellar between stars; most often used to describe travel from one star to another

lift upward force of air that causes an object to fly

membrane thin, flexible layer of tissue or skin

migration regular movement of animals as they search different places for food

radar device that uses radio waves to track the location of objects

thermal having to do with heat or holding in heat

thorax middle section of an insect's body; wings and legs are attached to the thorax

thrust force that pushes a vehicle forwards

READ MORE

Aircraft (Science and Technology), Andrew Solway (Raintree, 2012)

Fighter Aircraft (Ultimate Military Machines), Tim Cooke (Wayland, 2015)

Flight (Kingfisher Readers), Chris Oxlade (Kingfisher, 2012)

Frightful Flight (Horrible Science), Nick Arnold (Scholastic, 2014)

Planes and Helicopters: The History of Inventions (It'll Never Work), Jon Richards (Franklin Watts, 2016)

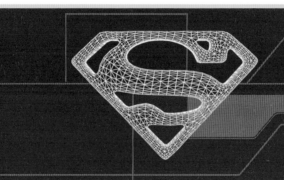

WEBSITES

www.bbc.co.uk/nature/life/Bumblebee#p007vs8p
Watch this fascinating video to learn more about how a bumblebee flies.

www.rafmuseum.org.uk
Have a look at The Royal Airforce Museum website. You could even go for a visit!

INDEX

aeroplane wings 7, 8–9

airfoils 8–9, 12, 20

air resistance 9

Alcock, John 11

Allen, Bryan 12

An-225 24

Arctic terns 18, 19

B-2 Spirit 23

bird wings 6, 8, 19

blowflies 21

Brown, Arthur 11

bumblebees 20

butterflies 20

cargo planes 24–25, 29

drones 26–27

eagles 7

flying fish 4, 16, 19

flying frogs 17

flying snakes 17

flying squirrels 17

Gossamer Albatross 12

gravity 6, 7, 28

hang-gliders 4, 12, 29

Harrier Jump Jets 23

helicopters 11, 23, 25

hot air balloons 27

hummingbirds 19

jet packs 14–15

lift 7, 8, 9, 12, 20

Lilienthal, Otto 8, 10

Mi26 25

migration 18, 20

RoboBee 21

Rossy, Yves 15

Sikorsky, Igor 11

sooty terns 19

spacecraft 28–29

spoilers 9

Springtail EFV 15

spy planes 22

SR-71 Blackbird 22

stealth aircraft 4, 22, 23

Super Guppy 25

thrust 6, 7, 15, 23, 28

Vinci, Leonardo da 10

Voyager 1 29

wingsuits 4, 13, 29

Wright, Orville 10, 11

Wright, Wilbur 10